DIVIDEND INVESTING

Mistakes to Avoid, Tips to Follow and Tricks to Keep Your Money in Your Pocket Where It Belongs

RICHARD BLOOM

© Copyright 2019 - All rights reserved.

The content contained within this book may not be reproduced, duplicated or transmitted without direct written permission from the author or the publisher.

Under no circumstances will any blame or legal responsibility be held against the publisher, or author, for any damages, reparation, or monetary loss due to the information contained within this book. Either directly or indirectly.

Legal Notice:

This book is copyright protected. This book is only for personal use. You cannot amend, distribute, sell, use, quote or paraphrase any part, or the content within this book, without the consent of the author or publisher.

Disclaimer Notice:

Please note the information contained within this document is for educational and entertainment purposes only. All effort has been executed to present accurate, up to date, and reliable, complete information. No warranties of any kind are declared or implied. Readers acknowledge that the author is not engaging in the rendering of legal, financial, medical or professional advice. The content within this book has been derived from various sources. Please consult a licensed professional before attempting any techniques outlined in this book.

By reading this document, the reader agrees that under no circumstances is the author responsible for any losses, direct or indirect, which are incurred as a result of the use of information contained within this document, including, but not limited to, — errors, omissions, or inaccuracies.

Table of Contents

Introduction

Getting rich is something that most of us are probably aspiring to; owning a huge mansion, having an exotic car collection and possibly even having a yacht, helicopter or private plane. Hollywood has illustrated what the world of stocks and shares looks like, and we have all received the message: this is the life, this is how you can get rich. However, this is just the tip of the iceberg, as not all people investing in stocks are getting rich. In fact, only a few of them can say that they are making huge money on the stock market, but there are also plenty of investors who are making a decent living from such investments. The question is: How can you put your savings to work for you and generate more income? If you are thinking of making a deposit into a bank account, and then being able to live off the interest you receive from the bank, this is not possible. You might receive a stable, passive income, but the interest barely covers the inflation rate, so you are not making that much money. Some people choose to invest in real estate, which truth be told, is not a bad choice, but it can also have downsides. Apparently, there are plenty of people investing in cryptocurrencies, but these kinds of investments are too risky for a real investor, and they are only making calculated risks. P2P lending seems to be the riskiest way to invest money nowadays, but FOREX is also something that a few investors really like to consider or are already trying. Most of these sorts of investments don't require too many numbers, are easier to understand, but they are also risky. A cautious investor will probably not even consider them. However, the Stock Exchange is where the money is, as most investors "play" on this market. You would probably be shocked by how much money passes through not only the Wall Street Stock Exchange, but also others worldwide like London, Frankfurt, Tokyo, Shanghai, Hong Kong, and Toronto. The life of a stock agent is pure madness, as he/she is always on the clock closing deals and accumulating fat commissions. Investing in stocks is simply not for everyone, as it involves too many numbers to look for, financial statements, graphics, and statistics. Also, it requires a larger amount of money, so it's simply something that not anyone can jump into. That's why the stock exchange is a more restrictive market, because you may not have a sufficient amount of money in your bank account, or simply don't have the knowledge and skills to invest in it. Still, the fascinating world of stocks is not a mirage for plenty of investors active in this domain. The stock exchange is just a fancy way to fund companies, by giving away a part of ownership, a share. As an investor, you can try to speculate the fluctuation of a share, buy it when it has a low value, and sell it when it has a much higher value. However, there is another way to make your money work for you. You can simply keep your shares and receive an income from having these shares. If the company (or companies) you have shares in is profitable, the management can decide to share the profits with all investors. The money you receive back as a result, in this case, can be a constant stream of passive income called dividends. Profitable companies are issuing dividends periodically to their investors (also known as shareholders), most of which are paid on a quarterly basis. Therefore, in each quarter, a company's board of directors can decide to distribute the profit to its shareholders. That's why they use a document called dividend declaration rate, in which they set the dividend amount to be spread among the investors. Only those ones with a dividend record rate are eligible to receive dividends from the company. Any savvy investor on the stock exchange would be interested in the dividend yield and the dividend payout ratio. When the latter indicator is between 40-50%, this can prove that the company distributes nearly half of its profits to shareholders. The rest of the profit may be used to decrease a short-term loan or to release a product. If investors are noticing a high dividend yield, then they can expect a large cash income.

Dividend investing is just a strategy to buy stocks that are usually issuing dividends as an effort to create a constant stream of passive income. This approach is for the investors that want to be on the stock market for the long term. Whether is just a sum of money he invested, so he/she can have in a few years and retire, or just money invested wisely to get a college education for his/her newborn child. Dividend investing is for the very cautious investor, the one that doesn't like to take too many risks. It allows the investor to benefit from the constant stream of passive income from his/her holding. There are plenty of reasons why investors should consider dividend investing and you can find the most important of them below:

1) Having a restriction on cash flow may lead to lower accruals. Every time an investor takes a look over the balance sheet or the income statement, they are not interested in the accounting techniques showed over there, as they are not interested in becoming accountants. However, they are very keen on checking the net present value

of the discounted cash flows that can be generated for the owners. When they are assessing a stock, they always consider the owner earnings, not quite the net income applicable to common. A company that is capable of paying dividends to its investors sends a strong message out there, it basically says that the investment paid off and continues to do so. If there are fewer modifications made to the accounting records, there is a higher “quality of earnings” and the reported profits coming up are close to the free cash flow calculated in a conservative manner. As it turns out, in the long run, companies that have lower accruals can beat companies with higher accruals when it comes to total return.

2) Funds for Managerial Allocation can be lower by a commitment to on-going cash. Having excess cash can lead to spending it on mergers and acquisitions of pension benefits, bonuses, higher salaries, stock options, and many other things. Paying dividends to the investors can mean less money to spend for managers, which in some cases tend to spend it on different things which are not generating income for investors. It can be a private plane or

benefits to employees. Mergers and acquisitions can be a very lucrative investment, but this doesn't mean that executives and managers will just have to jump into this process. They will need to be extremely selective with these situations, otherwise, they would spend the money on all sorts of companies, and this is not something recommended. If they are in such situations, they will have to compare the companies between themselves, and just select the best option and discard the other ones.

3) "Yield Support" when the Stock Market collapses. Let's consider that there is a company that set the share at $100 and pays a 3% dividend. Now, this looks like a very stable company, capable of paying very good dividends for its investors. However, the stock market has fluctuations and it can crash once in a while. Guess which companies will have the most investors? The ones paying handsome dividends of course. Even if the value of the share drops, because the dividend is not affected by this decrease in value, the investors will rally to support the company which pays best. This will increase the value of the share again, so

paying handsome dividends may reverse the drop in shares.

4) Return Accelerator. Supporting the Yield of the share can also lead to the phenomenon of "Return Accelerator" (named by Dr. Jeremy Siegel), which protects the shares from bear market effects. Reinvesting dividends back into the shares through the dividend reinvestment plan will simply create more equity to the shares. This is why the oil companies did a lot better in bear market periods than the rest of the companies listed on the stock exchange and were included in the S&P 500 stock market index.

5) Dividends offer a psychological advantage to some investors. For some people, the stock exchange is more about instinct and feeling, than reason and numbers. If a company offers dividends to its investors, this sends a message that the company is successful enough. Everybody likes to see that the investment pays off, so there is no better way of paying off your investment than receiving dividends from it. Some of the investors are not looking for speculations, to buy shares when they are

low and sell them when they are high. These kinds of investors are in the game for the long run, so they want to see their investment work. However, this doesn't mean that an investor should put all their eggs in one basket, as they need to diversify and invest in many other companies to lower the risk. However, they will need to make sure to buy shares that pay dividends. It's common sense, after all, dividend-paying stocks are a lot more attractive than the rest, so they are more likely to attract more investors.

If all of the above is not convincing enough, then you should check the advantages of dividend investing, as listed below:

- Get Paid to Wait. Investors decide to invest in such stocks because they are paid at regular intervals, so in other words, they are paid to wait. Dividends are simply a great way of getting ongoing return without having to wait for capital appreciation;

- Dividend Growth Compounding. Growing dividends have a positive impact on exponential growth. This happens because the dividends per share and number of shares are growing. The dividend growth compounding can work its magic without depending upon the stock value increases.

- Take Advantage of Bear Markets and Corrections. Some investors know that the best time to reinvest their dividends is during bear markets or corrections. That's when the price per share is lower. Increasing the number of shares means significantly boosting your dividend growth in the long term.

- Preserve Capital. Paying dividends to investors is a great sign that the company is stable and mature. This can encourage more investors to come on-board. The stocks of these kinds of companies will hold up a lot better during bear markets, compared to other speculative stocks. Dividend-paying stocks have something to buoy them when the market drops, but speculative ones simply don't and investors risk losing all their money;

- Create a Constant Income Stream. Wouldn't it be nice to get some money out of your investment? If investing in real estate can get you a constant income from rent, dividends can provide a regular income to the investor. Usually, the dividends are received every 3 months, but having a very complex portfolio of dividend-paying stocks can generate you an income a lot more frequently (even a monthly income). It's recommended to buy stocks that can sustain or even increase their dividends. Focusing just on the yield when purchasing stocks is foolish.

- Inflation Hedge. If incomes will not grow, the purchasing power will decrease over time, affected by inflation. Just an annual 3% inflation will chop out more than 50% of your purchasing power in less than 24 years. Dividend-paying stocks can represent the perfect way to alleviate the effects of inflation.

Chapter 1: Not Doing Enough Research

So far, we established that investing in dividend-paying stocks is one of the best strategies when it comes to a reliable income. After all, this is the difference between investor and trader. An investor is spending money to generate an income, whilst the trader is buying and selling shares for a living. Is it wise to put all eggs in one basket? Or is it fine to diversify your investment strategy and also buy stocks for yields? Most of the specialists would recommend diversity, so why not be part trader, part investor? You can benefit from both sides of stock investing, but it's best for you to have more money invested for dividend-paying stocks and less money for 'gambling' on the stock market with 'hot' stocks. In order to properly invest money in stocks and receive back dividends you will need to avoid some very common mistakes, and probably the most common mistake of all is **not researching enough**. Having just a pension plan will probably not be enough for your retirement, not if you have bigger plans. Inflation can be devastating on your accumulated pension, and the pension pot is usually managed by investment funds who tend to invest very cautiously in bonds and other safe avenues. These kinds of investments will not bring too much return and therefore will not have a significant increase in your pension fund. This is why you need to take matters into your own hands and invest in dividend-paying stocks. How much you will be able to increase your investment, it's up to you, but to maximize your dividends you will need to do thorough research first. Investing in stocks and receiving handsome dividends is not that easy. Otherwise, everyone would invest in it. You would probably see everybody investing in the tech giants, or famous companies or banks. However, these companies may not offer dividends, or if they offer, it will probably be very small. This is one reason why people are jumping in and buy these shares, whether we're talking about a big bank, huge retailer or giant tech company. The capitalization on these companies is unbelievably high, so buying shares at such companies will simply not have the results you are looking for. Such companies are usually looking to find a way to pay fewer taxes and they use their capital on development or other ridiculous investments. They simply won't value you too much as an investor, so you shouldn't expect too many dividends coming your way if you decide to buy these stocks. That's why investing in these 'elephants' may not be the best strategy. As these stocks are popular enough, you will need to look for the special ones, stocks of companies which are not quite known to the wide audience. Therefore, you will need to search for emerging companies, the companies that really want your money and are willing to reward you for investing with them. If you buy shares at Coca-Cola, Amazon, Wells Fargo, Walmart, and other giants then guess what, you won't see a spectacular income from them. You might as well let the investment funds manage your pension and investing in the safest bonds. Probably any investor is familiar with the S&P 500, which lists the largest 500 companies all over the US listed on NASDAQ, NYSE or BZX Exchange. As you probably expect, these companies are not that generous when it comes to paying dividends, as the profits are used for development, growth and other investments to strengthen the position of the company. There are plenty of investors that go straight for companies from this list because they are aware of them and they feel comfortable investing in them. However, you will need to look outside the S&P 500 list and find the "rising stars" on the stock market. As all the companies listed have published their financial statements which can be found when searching for the listed company on the stock market website, you can use the information to your benefit. You can have your own strategy to find emerging companies listed on the stock exchange, by searching the internet. Once you have a list (you probably need to have tens, if not hundreds of emerging companies), you should check the following aspects:

1) Dividend payout ratio (DPR) represents how much a company pays out its investors in dividends, compared to the stock earnings. To find out its value, you need to divide the annual dividends per share with the EPS. The DPR is an indicator of how much the company can support paying dividends from its earnings. Usually, a higher DPR is associated with a more mature company. It's a common belief for such companies that the best use for their profits is to give it away to their shareholders in the form of dividends. Growing companies may have fewer earnings (or none at all) to spend on dividends, that's why their DPR is lower or close to zero.

2) Dividend yield represents the return on a dividend, regarded as a percentage of the stock price. It's the ratio between the annual dividend per share and the price per share. If you are wondering what this

indicator is for, you should know that it shows the amount of cash flow you are getting for your money.

3) Earnings per share (EPS). This is an indicator which was already mentioned when calculating the DPR. The EPS represents the amount that each share would get if the company decides to pay all its profits to investors. There is a simple way to find out its value, by dividing the total profit of the company by the number of shares. As it happens, this is one of the best indicators that show how a company performs and how efficiently the money is spent. Also, you can use it to compare companies in the same field of activity. Usually, companies with steady and consistent annual growth are most likely to outrun other companies with volatile earnings.

4) Price to earnings ratio (P/E) measures the relationship between the stock price of a company and its earnings, and you can find out its value by dividing the price per share by the earnings per share. This can let you know if the stock price is too high or too low, compared to its earnings.

5) Price to earnings growth ratio (PEG) can help you understand the previous indicator a bit better, as you can calculate it by dividing the P/E ratio by projected growth in earnings (of the company). The PEG indicator can let you know if the stock you have may be of good value or not. If the number is lower, you will need to pay less in order to get in the expected future earnings growth of the company.

6) Price to book value ratio (P/B) can be used to compare the market value of the company, with the ones shown in the financial books. It represents the ratio between the current price per share and the value per share shown in the books. The book value represents the company's current equity, as shown in the yearly report. Usually, when the P/B is lower, it's actually better for you, as you pay less for more book value.

OK, so these are the figures you need to carefully study when you want to invest in dividend-paying stocks. However, you will not have to verify only the financial statements of the last year, as you will need to analyze them for a much longer period. Check the indicators above for bull or bear market periods, but also in terms of a financial crisis. As you need to expect at one point that the value of the stock will fluctuate, you have to be prepared for moments like a drop in the stock price. If you can find the data of a company for the past 25 years it can be very helpful for you. Of course, analyzing data for different companies is not a 5-minute job, as it takes a lot longer than that, but any serious investor needs to be informed properly in order to make a smart investing decision. By doing this, you should be able to find out the companies that have high respect for shareholders and pay them plenty of profit in dividends. It's said that's recommended to have around 20-30 companies to invest in from different "hot domains" of activity. However, in order to find those companies, you need to analyze a lot more companies and decide which one is better to invest in. If you can find out steady, reliable companies with decades of experience and paid dividends to their shareholders this is where you need to put your money. However, all companies can experience drops in their stock price, what is important is how they get over it. If the financial crisis situations are usually characterized by scared investors, who will simply not invest anymore because of the uncertain climate, wise investors know that's the perfect time to buy and grow their portfolio. If you watch financial news, you are probably seeing all kinds of analysts freaking out for mostly insignificant things, they are spreading the fear amongst most of the investors out there. That's why many of them are determined to sell, not making much profit or even having a loss, whilst other investors benefit from this situation, as they buy the shares at very low prices. Analyzing how these companies go through a financial crisis and how they handled these hiccups is very important. Investing in companies that reward their shareholders with generous dividends is the way to get through this uncertain period. When other investors are desperate to sell, a wise investor should be interested in buying, especially if it's a way to increase the number of dividends paid. Some investors use the money received from dividends to invest back in the stocks of the same company, so more shares will automatically mean more dividends. These are the investors that trust their feelings and ignore the hysteria of financial analysts forecasting the doom for one company or another. By continuing to invest in dividend-paying stocks you will be able to create over the years a valuable portfolio of Perpetual Dividend Raisers, that can generate you an increasing stream of wealth and income - with minimal work on your side. In fact, the only thing you need to worry about is doing the research properly.

Here's something you will need to consider, according to Ned Davis Research, the companies that raised or just initiated dividend payments from 1972 to 2010 did a lot better than the companies that didn't. After 38 years, the companies that cut dividends were at only $82 after the original investment of $100, having a compound yearly growth rate of -0.52%. The companies that didn't pay dividends were worth at $194, having a very small growth of 1.76% annual return. In the case of companies that paid dividends but kept it at the same value, the value was $1,610, with a 7.59% annual return. If $100 invested in these companies creates very different returns ($82 for companies cutting dividends, $194 for companies that didn't pay dividends and $1610 for companies that paid dividends at a constant value) over one year, you can see where the trend goes for the period of 38 years. As it happens, the same amount of $100 invested in dividend raising companies, or in companies that initiate dividend payment, is worth $3,545 and has an annual growth of 9.84%. The last option is definitely the right option to invest, but this doesn't mean that you can't get more than 9.84% in annual returns.

This is why you need to do your homework properly, and come up with the list of companies you can invest in. You will not find them in the S&P 500, so you definitely need to look beyond that list. Perhaps, you should choose the domain of activity first, but you don't have to stick to just one domain, as you can choose more. Tech companies can be very promising, but there are also other interesting domains to invest in. Once you have a few "hot domains", you would ideally have around 20-30 companies from each domain, all paying handsome dividends, and if possible, raising them. Having a diversified portfolio of stocks can significantly lower the risk you are exposing yourself to, as any company can have difficult times or may struggle to pay back its shareholders. This is why you need to diversify and not put all risk it all by investing all your money in one stock.

Chapter 2: Expecting Too Much Too Soon

Investing in dividend-paying stocks is something to look for in the long run, as you probably will not feel too rich in a few months. Think of it just like planting a seed, and letting it grow in the years to come. It can be the perfect retirement strategy if you are looking for an additional income. However, there are plenty of investors out there who are impatient and simply don't have the time to wait for an income. After all, with dividends, you are being paid to wait. But you will need to wait for an extremely long period of time, and see how money is being sent to you by the companies you invested in. You can do your normal job, and get additional money in return, just by having stocks at some companies you handpicked yourself. If your pension fund is managed by a company who decides to invest your money in the safest forms of investment, it can be bonds, different kind of stocks, or probably even real estate mutual funds, the money you will see added to your fund can barely cover the inflation rate. That's why you will need to take matters into your own hands and invest to have more money generated. If you want something done right, you have to do it yourself.

A handsome passive income is what most people dream of, but it takes a lot of preparations in order to generate it from dividend-paying stocks. As mentioned in the previous chapter, serious research has to be done, in order to pick the best stocks that pay dividends. However, once the homework is done, and you have increased your portfolio with 20-30 companies from each domain, then you can let the money work for you. But for how long you will have to wait until you see the results? Usually, companies pay dividends every 3 months, but if you have a diversified portfolio, it is possible to receive a monthly stream of dividends. Some investors may get discouraged when they see the first dividends coming in. They probably invested a handsome amount of money and they are noticing a minor amount of money returning. They might be disappointed, thinking that they could have made a better profit by selling their shares at a better price. If you are doing this, then you are more of a trader than an investor. You are basically looking for the quick and easy exit strategy, basically to sell your shares at a price better than the acquisition price. Under normal circumstances, you shouldn't do it, especially if the dividends you receive have a decent value. But wait, that's not all! As there are other forces at work in the long run, which can positively influence the money you get from stocks. You will also have to consider the yield on cost, which should normally stay above the inflation rate, and this can put some extra money in your pocket as well. However, what if you reinvest your dividends? What if you don't sell your stocks straight away and you can wait for money? If you plan to act like this in the long run, then you will earn big time on a long-term basis. You can even triple your money in the next ten years if you invest in dividend-paying stocks. Considering a stock that has 5% yield, increases the dividend rate by an average of 10%, and has a price that grows at 6% (which is below the 7.48% average increase for the S&P 500), such a stock can have a compound yearly growth of 12.34% over the next ten years. This means that an investment of $10,000 can turn into $32,028. But this is just for the next ten years, as time goes by, the results are even more spectacular. Only five years later, your $32,028 can almost double, turning into $62,754 and five years later it will double again, to $132,757 (at an annual compound growth rate of 13.8% and having a total return of 1,227%). Investing $10000 and then over 20 years getting back $132,757 may sound too good to be true, but this is totally possible. Also, this should make you think again if you want to cash out your stocks in a few months after buying them. It's still not convincing enough. What if you invest $100,000 and get back $1.32 million over 20 years? If you want to get this money by trading and speculating stock prices, it will require a lot of work, skills and also luck. It requires you to be active for a very long period of time, whilst investing in dividend-paying stocks can make you rich in 20 years, and all you need to do is sit back and enjoy life, whilst your stocks are appreciating and you are getting back dividends from them. This sounds like the easy way, but this is the investor way. Nobody says that you have to stick with the same number of shares for the 20 years period or longer. In fact, it's always recommended to reinvest your dividends in shares, to expand your portfolio and therefore create an increased income from dividends. You can even try to speculate with the price of some stocks if you have the time, skills and knowledge. See how that's working for you! However, most specialists would agree that having a larger part of your money invested in dividend-paying stocks is the right way. Once you already know some companies that reward their shareholders with handsome dividends, you can keep buying their shares, to increase the amount of money you receive from them in dividends. Trading shares can be a very difficult business but also investing in dividends is not quite the easiest thing you can do on the stock market. The risks may be higher when it comes to trading but the profits can be very handsome. Speculating with the price of stocks can reward you a lot, so you can make a jaw-dropping income out of this activity, but you need the skills, knowledge and proper understanding of the market. However, if you don't want to be on constant lookout for opportunities, then you will need to settle on some stocks which can provide a nice income. Even when you settle for these kinds of shares, you will need to make sure that you stick with them long enough and they pay dividends. You will need to set realistic expectations, so that you will know exactly how much money you will be receiving in dividends, and you don't get disappointed and sell the shares quickly. The best way to motivate yourself is to calculate for the long term, as the figures you can come up with will definitely make you want to stick to the stocks. You need to understand that the financial forecasts you can make can easily change, so nobody can guarantee those numbers. That's why, when you analyze a company that you want to invest in, it is better to dig as much as possible in the past. Find out the information you need like the DPR, EPS, PEG and so on. By studying the past, you can predict what will happen in the future. However, the unexpected can happen, like a change of management, too much debt, or the company may be struggling and experience difficult times. All these factors can prevent the company from offering dividends to its shareholders. If you study enough these indicators from their past financial records but also the current status, the information should be more than enough for you to make a decision and assume a calculated risk. Every company can experience its ups and downs, and you probably already noticed some moments like these if you study the financial statements over the past years. This is how you can find out the company's behavior towards its shareholders during lean times or good times. Whether you want to invest in the dividend-paying stocks of the company, and to keep them for a longer period of time, such information can influence your decision. Choosing this strategy can generate you a lot of passive income, as you need to keep in mind that this is a safe way to make money on the stock market. Usually, dividend-investing is a lot more beneficial for investors than trading stocks (buying them at a low value and selling them at a higher value), that's why it's better to keep the stocks for a long period of time (and receive money from dividends), instead of trading stocks.

Chapter 3: Losing Track of the Stock You Invest In

Handling a portfolio of stocks is not an easy thing to do, and there are plenty of investors out there who simply can't keep track of all their investments. In such situations, investors are overlooking (not on purpose though) some stocks which could have made them a nice income. Let's just say that you are an investor with plenty of stocks, and you probably don't keep track of all of them, or you may not be aware that you have bought some shares from a certain company. Or perhaps, you are doing this on purpose. You just purchase stocks and leave them unattended, until you decide to sell them when you think it's the right moment. This is not called investing, as it looks a lot more like gambling. When you simply ignore or forget about stocks, there is a high likelihood that it will not get you the biggest return (will simply not be the most profitable investment), also it will not let you know when it's the right time to buy or sell and you will not have any knowledge of how much return you have generated from these investments. You will need to keep track of every dime you invested in these stocks, in order to maximize your earnings and get more dividends. One consequence of ignoring a stock you invested in, is that you will never know how much dividends you are earning from that stock, so you can't plan accordingly to reinvest the dividends back into stocks. It's like having money in some pockets that you completely forgot about. You can imagine that you can't put this money to work for you unless you track them down and invest them wisely. Taking back control is probably an expression you hear a lot lately, but it also applies to the stock market. It can refer to gaining control over all your assets by monitoring them and using the investments in such a way to maximize your earnings. Not monitoring your stocks is like not having updated information about your investments, and a true investment needs to be based on specific information that can help you calculate the potential profit of a given stock (if it's worth the potential risk). The more you are able to keep track of your investments, the more data you have to use in order to maximize your income from your portfolio. You can't afford any cent to go to waste, that's why you will need to monitor the stocks properly and not leave anything out of your sight. This is why you will need to use sophisticated technology to monitor your stocks. Most of the major investors and bankers are aware of the importance of monitoring stocks, that's why in order to make sure they have everything monitored and controlled, they are using the best software out there. Such technology can easily monitor the entire stock market, as well as individual portfolios. Probably the most famous technology to track the stock market is Bloomberg Terminal, a very expensive software (it costs around $24,000 per year for a single unit) which can monitor the entire stock market. The general idea is that the game is played by very rich investors, they are making the rules and they are getting most of the profits from the stock market. However, using Bloomberg Terminal can give you the extra advantage that push you ahead of other investors, who may be new to the stock market and don't know exactly what they are doing. The info you can get from using this kind of software is very beneficial, and it can make a huge difference, but using this software is extremely expensive. Depending on the portfolio of stocks you have, you can decide if the software is worth it for you or not. You will probably need to have millions of dollars invested, to make sure that using this software is sustainable for you. Usually, this technology is used by those who can afford it, whether we are talking about investment funds, investment banks, or huge brokerage companies that handle plenty of clients with huge portfolios. As an investor, you will need to be very successful and have an extremely vast portfolio of stocks, with a value higher than a few million dollars, in order to make this technology worthwhile.

If you don't have the money for this kind of software, then you don't need to worry, as there are plenty of ways to monitor the stock exchange and your private portfolio free of charge. Although such software applications don't have the features of Bloomberg Terminal (not even close), you can still use these kinds of programs to successfully track the stocks you invested in. You simply can't expect to get so much data out of the programs, compared to Bloomberg Terminal, but they can still help you get a pretty clear picture of how your stocks are performing, in the short or long term. You can find plenty of apps out there (probably hundreds), not all of them may be free, but you can still use a few of them by paying a small or symbolic amount (they are a bit more sophisticated than the free ones). One of the most popular choices in terms of stock market monitoring is "Stockwatch", a software capable of providing very rich data of the stock market. Also, you can try Google Finance, that includes plenty of financial tools, including a stock market monitoring tool and a free portfolio management tool. Another interesting tool is Morningstar

Portfolio Tracker, capable of providing high-quality data on stocks for free. This tool also includes a transaction and a watchlist portfolio. These solutions can also come from promising startups like INDX.guru, as they can offer a very useful free solution of providing free information on stocks, but also on tracking new investors. Their sophisticated software has some very interesting features inspired by Bloomberg Terminal.

There is also the alternative of collecting data manually, an extremely time-consuming task, but at least you can make sure that there is no data left behind. You can simply collect all data from your portfolio, checking the internet for the latest updates on the stock market, or by simply collecting the data from the company itself. Then, you could collect new data by following the company's news feeds, Twitter, or just getting info from the most relevant channels to stock market investments.

Chapter 4: Being a Cheapskate

How much are you willing to invest in a dividend-paying stock? Are you prepared to go the extra mile to get your hands on the best stocks for dividends out there? Or you are interested in buying cheap stocks, just because you think they are great deals? Most investors are attracted like a magnet by stocks with very cheap prices, as they like to think that more is better. But they are not focusing on how much money that specific share can make for them. That's why they tend to waste their money on these kinds of stocks, and they will soon find out that these stocks are not performing well (in most of the times, as there may be some stocks out there that are incredible bargains). Other investors underestimate the earning potential of a stock, and they are simply not willing to buy the shares from such companies because they are expensive, ignoring some key indicators like DPR, EPS, PEG and so on. Instead of buying performant stocks, these investors spend their money on cheaper stocks, hoping that their stocks will appreciate or get some handsome dividends over time. However, there are plenty of traders out there, meaning they buy cheap stocks and they are selling them for a higher price, just to make a quick buck. There are too many naive investors and "dreamers" operating on the stock market, without basic knowledge of this market. Probably the least inspired investors are those ones that can see the potential in stock, they are aware how much dividends are going to receive from them, but they are not buying the stocks as they believe it's not worth it. It's OK to make your own calculations, but you still need to get the numbers right in order to maximize your investment. The ideal situation is to get a portfolio full of high-performance stocks, whether you spend more or less on these stocks. Anyway, the investment you will be making in these shares will pay itself off in a few years, so when you see really interesting dividend-paying stocks, you will always have to consider them for buying. Nobody says that you have to invest all your money in one stock, you definitely need to diversify your portfolio and invest in at least 20-30 companies. There are plenty of tools you can use and data you can analyze to make the right choice when it comes to purchasing dividend-paying stocks. That's why you will always need to compare stocks and only select the best of them to invest. You may have an approximate budget to invest, and the calculations you made (or the sum you estimated to pay on different stocks may be higher or lower). Since you compare stocks and you shortlisted a few of the best stocks out there (by analyzing EPS, DPR, PEG, and other indicators), you will need to invest more in the best stocks you selected, and less in the other stocks. Those ones which are the best may be more expensive than you anticipated, but this doesn't mean that you shouldn't invest in them, especially if the price is not too much higher than what you were prepared to pay for them. When you see the numbers rolling in and dividends paid back, you can congratulate yourself by making the right decision. Buying dividend paying stocks is, in fact, a calculated risk, so you can easily predict how much money your shares will generate for you. Perhaps you are exceeding your budget and may need to ask someone to lend you some more money. If you supplement your budget with a loan, most likely you will not regret it, as your dividends can pay off and make all the extra effort worthwhile. You don't have to fall in the trap of buying cheap stocks, just like you are buying clothes or shoes, as when it comes to investments, you will need to make every cent count. If you adopt this strategy, you can end up with a portfolio full of non-performant stocks, so you have a lot of money invested in these stocks, but not too much money coming out of them. This is a situation you will need to avoid, as this the path to failure or even becoming bankrupt. You will need to not judge a book by its cover (in this case, the price), as you need to dig deeper and find out everything possible regarding these stocks. Once you have your eyes set on some stocks paying handsome payouts (you will also need to judge if these dividends are sustainable for the long term), then it's very clear to you that you have to invest in these stocks. Buying cheap stocks is for rookies, the kinds of investors that spend their money on S&P 500 companies and on very cheap stocks, so they go from one extreme to another (very expensive to very cheap). There is a common ground for all these stocks, they don't pay too much of their profits to their shareholders. So, if you are set on investing money on dividend-paying stocks, why spend money on the S&P 500 companies or on extremely cheap stocks? You shouldn't worry too much about exceeding your budget if you want to invest in dividend-paying stocks, as you will come to see that you will quickly recover the extra amount you paid. However, if you are clever enough, you can still buy very interesting stocks for dividends at very good prices. But you will need to keep your eyes on the news. For instance, if a company announces a big dividend-payout on a certain date, you should start gathering as much information as you can on that company. If the shareholders are paid handsome amounts of money regularly, then you will need to wait until the company pays dividends and then buy shares at this company the next day. Most likely, the price will be discounted more than the standard price, so this is the best moment to get on board and become an investor at such a company. The big advantage when it comes to investing in these kinds of stocks, is that you truly know what you are buying, whilst with the cheap stocks it is incredibly difficult to get information related to them, so you don't know what you are buying. You can have your own sources to find the best dividend-paying stocks, but when you are scanning the stock market for the best stocks to invest in, always stay true to your principles:

- analyze the information before buying the stock, regardless if it's very cheap or a bit more expensive;

- don't jump to buy cheap stocks, as most likely they are not very productive;

- avoid filling your portfolio with too many cheap stocks that produce too little money back;

- go the extra mile and slightly exceed your budget if you find stocks that are worth buying;

- always invest more in the best dividend-paying stocks, and less in ones with lower potential.

A very good source of finding very interesting dividend-paying stocks is the Dividend Aristocrat list, so make sure you always have the list updated. You can also do your own research over the stock market, by selecting the sector first and then finding the best companies to invest in with a clear history of rising dividends over the years (decades, if possible).

Chapter 5: Becoming Distracted by Unreliable Sources

It's simply amazing how media can manipulate people and make them believe different kinds of news or stories. Some of you might call it propaganda, others think this is a bit exaggerated, but it's fair to consider that people are easily manipulated by media, especially when they are repeatedly exposed to the same source of news. We are bombarded by information, much of it which is fake since it has become too hard to distinguish fake news from real news. Just because a story is repeated too many times doesn't mean that it's true, but it can become accepted. Everything happens so fast that most people are not able to stop, think and analyze the news, to establish if it's true or not. There are too many sides to a story, and it has become extremely difficult to find the correct one. This is what's happening with news that we see on any news channel, related to politics (mostly), different events and other interesting stories they are showing nowadays. Such news is only meant to shock people, to spread panic amongst them as they often overexaggerate. This is why we are seeing "Breaking News" with most of the occasions, even though there isn't anything that interesting happening. Unfortunately, media sources for the financial market and stock exchange also use the same pattern. They tend to overexaggerate every time something is happening, so they are extremely dramatic when there is a minor hiccup on the stock market, or they are way too optimistic in case something good happens. Whether you find this news on TV, on the internet in the form of articles, podcasts, blogs and even on social media, it's very difficult to resist them and not to fall into this trap. Most investors are like a flock of sheep, they are easily manipulated by any kind of news. There may be some very high interest (and I don't mean bank interests) over the stock market, that spreading news which is not quite accurate or true has become something absolutely normal. The stock market analysts also play a major role, as they can easily influence a lot of investors out there. They usually exaggerate about stocks and spread panic amongst the investors. It's often said that if you have the information, then you are a rich man. Nowadays, you need to have the right information to become rich, because if you follow false information, you may lose a lot of money. Most investors are driven by the thrill of the moment, or the "gut feeling" to invest. They are investing after receiving an impulse, which can come from the media or from people they know. You will need to distinguish yourself from such investors, step out from the crowd, or from the "flock" (if you like), as you will need to be more rational. "Reading between the lines" is something that you will need to do because there are plenty of questions to be asked when analyzing news. You will need to find the cause of what's happening, what will be the consequences on the short, middle or long term, in order to better understand the news. Some news can be predicted, so you know exactly what will happen. A sudden decrease in the oil barrel can negatively influence companies that are in the oil business. If the President of the United States decides to raise the taxes on imports, you will need to know if you have companies in your portfolio who are importing from China, EU or other markets. Prices will most likely tend to fall. If a financial analyst overreacts on TV regarding certain stocks, you will need to double check the information first, as it may not be correct. When these analysts are spreading panic on the stock market, most investors will start to sell their stocks, and there will always be someone to benefit and buy good shares at a lower price, as these investors are desperate to sell. When all the analysts on TV are preaching financial crisis, most investors will panic and will start to sell their stocks at a lower price. Regardless of what these analysts are saying, these periods are the best times to invest in the stock market. Everything is a lot cheaper and you can easily expand your portfolio during such harsh times. Whilst other investors are cashing out, you can consolidate your position in the market and increase your portfolio. This is how you increase the number of shares, and more shares automatically mean more dividends. Investors are so easily influenced by all of these so-called "prophets". Always try to be more rational and analyze the news properly. Try to learn more about the stock market, find out how it works, and analyze all the possible facts. This is how you can determine if it worth panicking or not. Even when the worst is about to happen, you will need to keep your calm, as this is how you can come on top, whilst the others are falling.

Chapter 6: More Common Mistakes Made by Investors When Investing in Dividends

Dividends may not represent the winning strategy if you are investing incorrectly. It can make miracles for you, in terms of generating a healthy and handsome income, it can also substantially increase the value of your stocks over the years but all of these can be achieved if the investor follows a few principles and avoid making some mistakes, like the ones mentioned in the previous chapters. This chapter should provide you more info and insights on the mistakes you will need to avoid for future reference if you want to become a successful dividend investor. You can consider this chapter a guide on how not to invest in dividend-paying stocks. Below you can find some other mistakes that are made by plenty of investors today:

1) **Hunting towering yields**. You might be tempted to think that the stocks with the highest yields are very performant, but that's quite the opposite, as very high dividends are very difficult to sustain, or are

even unsustainable. This may lead to funds shortage when it comes to growth and development. Most specialists would recommend not to become blinded by extremely high yields, but to also check the dividend payout ratios. Studies can indicate that most performant stocks combine relatively low payouts ratios and not very high dividend yields. According to David Ruff, the sweet spot of the payout ratio is in the 30% - 60% range, which is a percentage that companies can easily commit to deliver on a regular basis to their shareholders.[1] Such payouts shareholders can easily reinvest in stocks for internal growth.

2) **Having mechanical strategies**. You will not have to base your strategy on the biggest numbers that show up, as some stocks were showing incredibly high dividend payout ratios or very attractive yields. Don't get blinded by these numbers and rush in to buy such stocks, as you need to filter more information to analyze these

[1] Hanson, J. (2013, June 19). 7 Big Mistakes to Avoid in Stock Dividend Investing. Retrieved from https://www.thinkadvisor.com/2013/06/19/7-big-mistakes-to-avoid-in-stock-dividend-investin/?slreturn=20190524191739

stocks. Extremely high dividend payout ratios are not sustainable for a long time, so you may need to avoid them;

3) **Ignoring growth factors**. Instead of concentrating just on dividend yields, you should also take into consideration aspects like capital appreciation and potential dividend growth. These are some key facts that any investor should focus on. If an investor has $1 million in its portfolio and wants to take out $50,000 per year to support his/her living expenses. With just 3% annual total return in 20 years, the investor would have less than half of his/her initial amount of $1 million, whilst another investor would have more than $1.8 million with an annual total return of 7%. In 30 years, the investor with 3% in annual return will deplete the money, whilst the other one would have more than $3 million. This is why potential dividend growth and appreciation are extremely important.

4) **Focus just on the home market**. Who says that you only have to invest at home? You can also search for other emerging or more favorable markets, as the average dividend yields tend to be a lot higher

overseas and stock valuations can be more advantageous.

5) **Blue-chip tunnel vision**. Just think of a poker table, where you have on the table chips of different colors. You have white chips, red chips, but the blue chips are the most valuable. Blue-chip companies are the most famous and most capitalized companies. Although investors may feel a lot more comfortable with the dividend stocks of famous large companies, these kinds of stocks have become way too expensive and have generated a lower return than other mid- or even small-cap dividend payers.

6) **Following the herd.** Many investors will feel tempted to invest in the huge large-cap stocks available on the market, but as shown above, they are not the most performant ones. You should ignore the trend and focus on finding small and mid-cap stocks that have a lot better performance than the large-cap ones. Whilst most investors are ignoring the potential of these lesser-known stocks, you shouldn't make the same mistake.

7) **Giving too much importance to macro**

factors. You shouldn't ignore other markets or emerging markets just because the nations hosting those markets are going through a difficult time. This doesn't mean that there aren't very good companies operating in these markets, companies that have potential. After all, this is a global market, if a company operating in a country does a lot of exporting, or works with companies from abroad, then that specific company is not too influenced by the national politics or economy. A good example would be the crisis of some countries from Europe, which shouldn't lead you to judge a book by its cover, as you can find plenty of reliable and solid companies over there.

8) **Searching for dividends in the wrong places.** People who want to invest in the stock market and to have a handsome income from dividends are often searching for them in the wrong places. They are not even selecting the right domain of activity or sectors, so it's very difficult for them to achieve the objective that they are pursuing. Perhaps a too common mistake is that these investors want to invest in giant tech companies, or other giant companies that

are more concentrated on growth and expansion, not quite on rewarding their shareholders with handsome dividends. These companies are too mature, so they are not very attractive in terms of dividend payout ratio, but people are more comfortable investing in these stocks, as they trust the brand. However, this is like investing in safe bonds, as they don't have the highest returns. As an investor, you will need to search for different opportunities, so you will need to look outside the S&P 500. The first step, you will need to select the sector of activity, it has to be a "hot" one, and only then try to find the best companies to invest in this sector. Usually, you will need to look for the small and mid-cap stocks, as they can provide you more generous dividends. You can also check The Dividend Aristocrats list, as this is one of the best sources for these kinds of stocks.

9) **Not reinvesting the dividend payments when possible.** Some investors may not be very satisfied with the dividends they are receiving, and therefore they might be thinking of abandoning this strategy. That's why they use the money received from dividends on something else,

like different living expenses, or buying stocks to trade. However, investing back the dividends in stocks will increase the number of shares you have. Long story short, more shares will mean more dividends, so more money. This is the safest way to increase your passive income, that's why every time you have the possibility, reinvesting the dividends is the most recommended thing to do to increase your passive income.

10) **Misjudging your financial need.** Every time you purchase stocks, you are actually taking a risk. If you are in desperate need of cash, this doesn't mean you have to make rash decisions, as you need to keep in mind that dividend payouts should not replace your salary or should cover your living costs. If you run the numbers wrong, this can be very devastating for you, as this situation may be a result of overestimating the income from dividends or underestimating expenses. Therefore, you will need to carefully consider your future needs, as this will play an essential role in your strategy. If the bar is set too high, you raise the odds of failing.

11) **Misusing a dividend strategy.** People

are often attracted by high numbers, so adopting a strategy that promises to deliver extraordinary results will be most likely their strategy. However, it may not be the winning strategy, as setting the bar too high can lead to disaster, therefore you should customize your own strategy when it comes to investing in dividend-paying stocks, as choosing an inappropriate strategy can be very dangerous. When selecting your strategy, you will need to fully understand your financial situation, the cash flow requirements, or personal balance sheet, as you need to determine the risk you are assuming in order to achieve your objectives.

12) **Trying dividend investing on your own.** The world of stocks is a wild jungle, where only the best can survive. Some investors require guidance to make it through this world. During your research, you will also need the opinion of a specialist, as you will need an expert's opinion when running through all the numbers. It can be someone from your family or a professional you ask for guidance. However, anyone helping you with these numbers will need to understand

first your objectives, your needs and the budget you are willing to spend on such investments. When it comes to making financial forecasts, or any kind of predictions, nobody can predict exactly what will happen on the stock market, or what will happen with the price of a share, however, having someone with knowledge of the stock market on your side can help you achieve your objectives and can help you become a successful investor.

13) **Purchasing a stock based only on a hot tip.** You can't just buy stocks because somebody tells you to buy them without doing your own investigations (or proper research). Some investors choose to buy stocks like this, considering that this is an inside tip, and you need to jump on the offer (the price of the stock) and buy it now before it gets a lot more expensive. This means acting without judging what will happen, as you might buy a stock without knowing basic information about the company like DPR, PEG, and EPS. The way to proceed in this case is to check the financial statements and also speak with one of the company's representatives (but at least your broker), to check if the tip you

received is the right information.

14) **Buying and selling shares just for the sake of dividends.** What if you buy a stock on one day, and the next day the company pays out the dividends for the shareholders? You collect your money and then sell the stocks at a very good price. This strategy should beat the market, as you win money from dividends and from the difference in price. Sounds too good to be true? Well, you can rest assured that pulling out this stunt is not possible. You may buy the shares on one day, get the dividends the next day, but if you plan to sell, the price of the share is lower because the company has publicly announced the big-time dividend payout. Therefore, you will not be winning anything if you sell immediately after receiving the dividends, as the most positive scenario would be to break even.

15) **Purchasing stocks just because they are cheap.** Some investors are attracted by low prices of stocks, just like when they are buying clothes. They feel like they just got their hands on the hottest deal out there. However, there is a huge difference between good value and low price per share, as if a share is cheap, this doesn't necessarily

mean it's a bargain. That's why buying stocks just because they are cheap can't be considered investing, it's, in fact, speculating or betting. You should ask yourself how can a low-priced share can help you, how it can generate money for you? Very cheap shares are often associated with unknown companies, the kind that you can't find too much information on them. Unless you see some financial statements, and also some clear indicators that fit your objectives, you shouldn't jump to buy cheap shares.

16) **Holding to a poor-performing stock for way too long.** The whole purpose of investing in dividends is to hold on to the stock to generate money for you. However, it doesn't mean to hold on to it no matter what. If you are stuck with a non-performing stock (which is not generating you enough income), then you definitely need to get rid of it. If you are already on a losing path and you are hoping that somehow the stock can still get generate money, you need to know that this is a losing strategy. If you are already emotionally attached to it, then it's a lot more complicated, as you stubbornly refuse

to let go of it. Emotional attachment, in this case, can be your biggest enemy, as you need to cut your losses, get rid of your shares (you will lose money again, but you will still get something in return) and invest your money in different stocks.

17) **Failing to account properly for taxes.** Most investors focus on how much money they are getting out of the stock market, which is something admirable, but how many of them are thinking of how much money they keep? This is a very important question, as income from the stock market have to be properly documented to pay lower taxes. A skilled accountant can make a difference in this case. You may earn $200,000 and pay 35 percent in taxes, so you remain with $130,000. If you pay only 15 percent taxes, you can walk away with $170,000. So, make sure you have a skilled accountant on your side, as you can walk away with more money if you have the proper consulting.

18) **Giving too much credit to analyses and media reports.** Just like any other domain, the stock market can have its very own news. There may be several channels, websites, magazines or TV and radio shows

related to this topic. Some of them can be excellent sources of information, whilst some of them may not be always right. Some analysts overexaggerate when it comes to the stock market, so you need to not give in to their hysteria and try to find as much information as possible, in order to confirm if the news is real or not. If you can't find information to prove the analyst's point of view, then you can simply continue with your dividend investing strategy.

Chapter 7: Disadvantages of Investing in Dividend-Paying Stocks

Not everything is perfect and investing in dividend-paying stocks is no exception. Most specialists can agree that you shouldn't invest all your money in these kinds of stocks, as you also need to diversify and play the role of a trader from time to time. If anyone invested in stocks just to hold on to the stocks, the entire stock market would be very boring. If you don't want to have spectacular income, just a steady predictable one, you should just invest in dividends. However, most investors would like to experience the thrills of trading. You can find below some disadvantages of this strategy, or why choosing to invest just in dividends can be an investing error.

1) Uncompensated risk. One of the issues with using this strategy for investing is that there are plenty of investors who only focus on individual stock investing. Having all your eggs in one basket is a very risky business, so in order to alleviate the risk, you will need to diversify your portfolio. The

uncompensated risk is, in fact, a risk that can be easily diversified away. Holding a portfolio of more than 10-20 stocks can be a great deal but investing in just 5 or 10 stocks means accepting too many individual stock risks. Buying a low-cost, very-diversified index fund (that the investor will simply not get compensated for it), can help to diversify the risk away. Therefore, why invest in stocks that have risks you can't get paid for? After all, investing can be all about risk control. Picking stocks is not an easy job to do, but if you choose to pick your own stocks you will have major risks to consider. Even the professionals handling millions of dollars can't pick the stocks well enough, so there are lower chances that an individual investor will do a better job;

2) Not focusing on total return. When purchasing stocks, most investors only focus on the yield, dividend, and income of the investment, but they are rarely thinking of the total return. If you consider 2 stocks, one with a 10% yield, whilst the other one has a 0% yield, you are probably considering going for the 10% one because it's a lot more attractive. Well, this is just the cover of the book, as these facts may be

misleading. Real Estate Investment Trusts are famous for being these kinds of stocks. Although they have an 8% yield, investors discovered that their shares only worth $3, and not $10 per share, the amount that investors originally paid. As it happens, a big part of the yield was considered as a return of their principal, but the total return is what matters most.

3) Confuse Dividend Stocks with Bonds. Just because dividend stocks can provide a regular income, this doesn't mean that they should be considered like bonds. You need to understand that nothing is for sure in the stock market, even solid companies that are paying dividends can go bankrupt. If bonds are considered as a loan, so a debt that has to be paid, dividends are something else completely. The value of the dividends can vary over time, so even companies like GE can cut their dividends to 1 cent per share. When the financial crisis occurred in 2008, there were plenty of dividends out there that were cut. More than 100 companies from the S&P 500 cut down their dividends back in those days. However, this was not the case with bonds, which kept their yields and even increase in value. A very relevant

example is the comparison between Vanguard Intermediate Treasury Fund which increased with 13.49% in 2008, whilst the Vanguard High Yield Dividend ETF decreased with 32.73%. You can imagine that the returns in these two cases are extremely different.

4) Dividends Are Not Tax Efficient. Usually qualified dividends are taxed at a lower rate than the ordinary income, but distributing the dividends are not quite good for investors. Some companies or investment funds like Berkshire-Hathaway (Warren Buffett's Investment Fund) have never paid any dividends. If there are no dividends being paid, the investor can decide when to pay the taxes on their shares from the company's portfolio. An investor can declare dividends every time he/she wants, by selling some shares. However, when there is no income declared, no taxes have to be paid.

5) An Inefficient Method in Order to Get a Value Tilt. Some investors would consider that a company paying dividends can determine the company to focus more on earning profits for its investors. The investors often consider that the dividends

are a lot more real than any increase in the price of the share. Also, they can provide historical data that shows how well the dividend-paying stocks are performing compared to other general stocks. But they don't point out why exactly this is happening. As it turns out, dividend-paying stocks were generally value stocks in the past, and during those times, these value stocks had significantly higher returns compared to the overall market. It's still not clear if this outperformance was caused by investor behavior, or it was just increased risk (or probably both), but it's very clear that investors steer their portfolio towards value stocks in order to benefit from them. Chasing high dividends may not be the best way to achieve this goal, as investors usually used a Price to Books ratio to steer their investing in the right direction (for value stocks). Therefore, if an investor chooses to avoid major and uncompensated risk, by purchasing an ETF or a low-cost dividend stock index fund, then the investor will probably be better off with a simple value index fund or an ETF instead. Investing in dividends is not a practice to be avoided, but you need to make sure that you diversify enough by buying stocks from 20-

30 (or even more) companies, focus on the total return, use dividends properly and make sure you still remain with something from them after taxes. Some investors choose to own these dividend-paying stocks by investing in market index funds or in ETFs. Whether you choose to buy them directly, it's up to you, but you should consider all of the above when choosing this strategy.

Chapter 8: What Are the Dividends to Invest In?

So far, this book has mostly included most of the mistakes which should be avoided, if you choose to invest in Dividend-Paying Stocks. However, there is still one topic left uncovered: what you need to consider in terms of numbers when choosing this strategy (dividend yields and dividend value). When evaluating these stocks, you will always need to consider the dividend yields over 4%, as they are the best in this case. However, don't be fooled by very high dividend yields (more than 10%), as these dividends tend to be extremely dangerous and not sustainable. Very high dividend yields might indicate that investors are selling the stock, lowering the price per share and raising the dividend yield as a result. You can choose the dividends you want to invest in by comparing the dividend yields amongst them. If you find a company that has a much higher dividend yield compared to others, this can indicate a red flag. You can also investigate further and look through the financial statements and previous history, just to find out if something fishy is going around.

Another indicator you will need to consider is the payout ratio of the stock, which can show you how much of the company's profit is going to its shareholders. If the payout ratio is too high (this is generally above 80%, but it can vary from a sector to another), this means that the company spends a large percentage of the profit to rewards its shareholders. You are probably asking: and what's the problem with that? They are just being generous with their investors. For starters, such a company pays back most of the profit in dividends, so there is no money left to be invested in the company's growth and expansion. A very high payout ratio can also mean that the dividend is not sustainable, so the company may struggle in the near future to keep the same levels of dividends. Going into debt is not a solution to pay the dividends a company owes to its shareholders.

A very popular practice amongst investors is to spend their money in dividend exchange-traded funds (ETFs), instead of individually selecting the high paying dividends stocks through comprehensive research. You have to picture the ETF as a bundle of securities all gathered into one investment. Obviously, the dividend ETF is all made up of dividend stocks. Such an instrument can allow you to purchase a very big selection of individual dividend stocks, all in one transaction.

It's a lot easier for investors to invest in ETFs or other kinds of funds than to invest in individual stocks. These funds can offer already what they should pursue when investing in dividends: diversification and a reliable and constant stream of income. When you already have a diversified portfolio of dividend-paying stocks, when a company decides to cut its dividends, the loss of income will be somehow alleviated (or even compensated) by other dividend-paying stocks you own in the ETF. We have to admit it, the stock exchange is a wild jungle, where most of the investors can't make it out on their own. They don't have enough knowledge of the market, they can't conduct proper research to find out most of the details you are interested when searching for so many companies, and they lack the skills or knowledge to properly analyze the data found through the research. This is why they need the proper guidance to find out the best opportunities on the stock exchange. Brokerage companies can help you in this situation, as you will need to compare yourself to a blind person, and the brokerage companies are the guide dogs to help you walk through this market. Some of the best-rated brokerage companies are Ally Invest, Ameritrade and E Trade. When you open an account with them, there are several things you will need to consider, like the trade fee, the minimum requirements of invested amount (or account minimum), but also a promotion might influence you to start your adventure on the stock market with one of these brokers.

Below, you will find a list of the hottest dividend-paying stocks, some of the dividends are calculated at a value which is below $1 per share. Usually, companies pay dividends to their shareholders every quarter.

Symbol	**Company Name**	**Dividend Yield**	**Dividend**
HPT	Hospitality Properties Trust	7.62%	$0.53
T	AT&T Inc	6.54%	$0.51
GEF/B	Greif Inc.	5.54%	$0.65
BCE	BCE Inc.	5.46%	$0.79
STX	Seagate Technology Plc	5.36%	$0.63

CMP	Compass Minerals International Inc.	5.29%	$0.72
PM	Philip Morris International Inc	5.23%	$1.14
UVV	Universal Corp	4.99%	$0.75
OXY	Occidental Petroleum Corp	4.73%	$0.78
QCOM	QUALCOMM Inc.	4.66%	$0.62
CM	Canadian Imperial Bank of Commerce	4.59%	$1.36
D	Dominion Energy Inc	4.56%	$0.9175

IBM	International Business Machines Corp	4.50%	$1.57
BNS	The Bank of Nova Scotia	4.34%	$0.85
IP	International Paper Co	4.27%	$0.50
PRU	Prudential Financial Inc	4.21%	$1
MDP	Meredith Corp	4.03%	$0.575
PFG	Principal Financial Group Inc.	4.02%	$0.54
RY	Royal Bank of Canada	4.01%	$0.98
EIX	Edison International	3.98%	$0.61

CVX	Chevron Corp	3.98%	$1.19
SLF	Sun Life Financial Inc	3.92%	$0.50
AVGO	Broadcom Inc	3.83%	$2.65
KSS	Kohl's Corp	3.79%	$0.61
TGT	Target Corp	3.54%	$0.64

[2]

[2] O'Shea, A. (2019, June 18). High-Dividend Stocks: 25 Stocks That Pay High Yields. Retrieved from https://www.nerdwallet.com/blog/investing/high-dividend-stocks/

Chapter 9: Frequently Asked Questions

What kind of companies can pay dividends?

Companies that are listed on the stock exchange market and have steady or growing earnings can pay dividends. Dividends simply can't lie, as it's a financial reward for the investor, but also an indicator that the company is doing well. Companies that pay dividends are associated with lower risks. As an example, when the price per share drops, the dividend yield can increase and attract more investors (this is a dividend support program).

Where I can find the companies that pay dividends?

Since there are more than 16,000 stocks in the US, it is very difficult to scan manually, analyze and decide which stocks are worth the investment, in order to receive dividends. You can use all sorts of tools and the latest technology, but a good starting point is the Dividend Aristocrats list or the list from the previous chapter.

Why it is important to invest in dividends?

All the stats indicate that dividend-paying stocks represent more than 40% of the overall market, so why miss out such an important chunk of the market's return?

When are dividends paid?

Companies can declare and pay dividends on a quarterly, semi-annual or annual basis, but they can also have special one-time payouts of dividends.

How to calculate the dividend yield?

This indicator represents the ratio between the total annual dividends paid per share and the current price per share. If a company has an annual dividend of $2 per share and the price of the share is $40, this leads to an annual dividend yield of 5%.

Why should you concentrate on dividends?

Dividend-paying companies are less risky compared to other companies that have never paid a dividend. Dividends mean actual cash and they simply can't be manipulated (unlike the earnings). Dividends are always considered the more stable part of total returns, and they are also positive, which makes them the ideal type of investment for people about to retire. Paying out dividends can be a challenge for the management of the company, as they need to properly assess the cash flow and only focus on the best ideas, whilst keeping enough cash to pay the shareholders. Since the company is paying dividends, management will be restrained from using the money for growth and development (through their own forces), or for mindless acquisitions or mergers. Cutting down dividends can send a very strong message that the company is too weak to handle itself financially.

What to look for in a dividend stock?

You can set your own rules when it comes to the levels of the indicators you are looking for. However, you should always consider investing in companies that have increased dividends over time, the P/E ratio should be below 20, the yield over 2.5% and the dividend payout ratio (DPR) just below 60%. These are just some recommended levels, which you can break from once in a while, just to take a higher risk.

How to handle dividend payments?

In the accumulation phase, it's wise to re-invest the money you received from dividends. As an example, if you save between $1,000 and $2,000 from dividends, you can reinvest the money to buy some shares in a company which is very attractive (assuming that you have done very comprehensive research related to the stock market). You can target the companies with 6%-7% of annual dividend growth, correlated with a 3%-4% yield, to get a 10% increase of the annual dividend income.

When is the right time to sell a dividend stock?

You can sell a dividend stock right after a dividend cut, when the company was acquired by a different company or when you decide that the company's shares are overvalued, for the growth you expect out of it.

Are dividends being paid on a monthly or annual basis?

As far as we are aware, there might be some companies in the US that pay dividends on a monthly basis. Usually, companies are paying them every 3 months, every 6 months, or even once per year. It depends on the company's policy. In other words, if a company pays $2 annual dividends per share, and you own 30 shares, you will receive $60 per year.

Can I consider dividend stocks to be safer?

As a matter of fact, dividend-paying stocks should not be considered safer than other stocks, as it can be just as risky as the rest of them. Companies are paying out their profit to their shareholders, but they still need to grow or expand. Nothing is certain on the stock market, as one day, the management of a dividend-paying company just decides to cut down on dividends because the money is not performing that well and they can barely keep up with the operating expenses. Maybe they are barely paying their employees, and their cash flow was reduced lately. Or perhaps, the management decides to invest the profits in the development of the company, in its growth or expansion, so they have to cut down on dividends, or just skip paying them. These scenarios can happen to all kinds of dividend-paying companies, that's why these stocks are not as safe as you probably think.

Conclusion

It's very clear that the world we live in requires more money, as there are plenty of temptations out there, which can empty your wallet and your bank account. Unfortunately, almost nobody is keen on saving money, as most people live in debt, work 2-3 jobs to pay their mortgage and other debts. Clearly, this lifestyle can lead you to the madhouse, as something has to change to relieve yourself from these shackles. Saving money and depositing it into a bank account is clearly not the best way to get a handsome return on your money. Some people already tried different types of investment, more or less risky, to generate more income for them. Whilst others prefer to invest in real estate, some other people prefer much higher risks and like to gamble their money by purchasing cryptocurrencies (Bitcoin is probably the most famous one), playing with currencies from all over the world on the Forex market, or lending money on P2P platforms. There are many "so-called" investors playing with fire and trying to make tons of money by using the methods mentioned above. You can see the ads on the internet or on social media, or people bragging that they made lots of money in just one day. Since people are desperate to get an extra income, they foolishly jump in and spend money using these methods, only to be very disappointed afterward. Other people are stuck in an MLM structure, desperate to get more affiliates in order to get more money. Such methods are very confusing, that's why most people don't get too much money out of it. You probably have better chances of winning the lottery than becoming successful using these methods. What you need instead is a method that has been proven to generate a nice income for the investors using it. Something that makes sense and can be understood (if it's properly researched). Although it's an enigma for the wide audience, the stock market can provide an interesting and sustainable approach to get an additional income. Most people are confused by this market, but it's slowly becoming more popular, as the companies present on this market are becoming more attractive to invest in. Just like owning real estate and renting it to get an income, you can get a reliable and constant income from the stocks you purchase. There are 2 types of people in the stock market. You have investors, who are willing to spend money on stocks, hold on to them and get money back when the company decides to distribute the profits. The other type is represented by the traders, who simply buy stocks at a low price and sell them back when the time is right at a higher price, in order to get a profit. This approach on investing is a lot more active, and as soon as you have sold the stock, you will have to scan the market for new opportunities. The investor approach has its main purpose to generate a passive income for the stocks he/she owns. Studies have shown that dividend-paying stocks are performing a lot better than the rest of the stocks, so this can be an extra reason why investors should consider investing in them. Finding the right stocks to invest in is not an easy task, as you will need to analyze indicators like EPS (earning per share), DPR (dividend payout ratio), the value of the dividends, but also the dividend growth rate or total return. If you are skilled enough, then you know how to avoid the traps like way too high DPR, high yields with small return rates and so on. You will always need to ask yourself if the company can support paying the dividends for a longer period of time, as some of them are luring the investors with extremely attractive DPRs, which are simply not sustainable for a longer period of time. The secret of making the right decisions lies within the research you will need to conduct on the stocks you want to buy. This is when you have to be very selective, as you have to create a list of 20-30 stocks that you will need to own, after ruling out several others (tens, if not hundreds of companies). This is a very time-consuming task, but if you have the passion for it, and also the skills and the knowledge you should be able to come up with a very interesting list of stocks. Now that you have the list, you only need to invest in these stocks and watch them do their work for you and generate you an income. Usually, companies pay out dividends every 3 months (the ones that truly value their shareholders), so you can quickly see some results. However, you will need to be patient with investing in dividend-paying stocks, as the more you hold on to these shares, the more money they will generate for you over time. Releasing them too soon may not be the best strategy because you can gain more money if you keep your money invested in the stock. Once you start receiving dividends, the best way to spend them is to reinvest them again in stocks, to grow your portfolio of performing dividend-paying stocks. More shares will automatically mean more dividends for you. Investing in dividends seems to be the ideal investing strategy for persons who want to retire. They don't have the time to be always on the stock exchange looking for more opportunities. Such investors are looking for a reliable and constant income, to come as extra cash in addition to their pension. If manually picking the stocks to invest in is way too difficult, you can just invest in ETFs as they have plenty of dividend-paying stocks in their portfolio. Diversifying the portfolio is another key to your success when targeting dividends because you will significantly lower the risk you are exposing yourself to. Fluctuations are something absolutely normal on the stock exchange, so companies may experience sudden drops when it comes to the price of the share. This can impact the value of the dividend, but if your portfolio is diversified enough, then you will not be too exposed to the risk. As the stock market is a jungle, you need consultants on your side to guide you through the market and advise you on the stocks you will need to buy. There are several brokerage companies out there, which you can hire to help you with investing in stocks. You will need to carefully examine their portfolio and fees, before registering with them. This book can advise you how to avoid the most common mistakes of investing in dividend-paying stocks, by providing very valuable tips and tricks for this kind of investment strategy. Learning from mistakes can be the best way of learning, but when you fully understand the downsides of this method and you also find out how to discover and evaluate the dividend-raising stocks, it can only give you an extra motivation to read this book.

References

6 Dividend Investing Mistakes - And How to Avoid Them. (2017, July 01). Retrieved from https://seekingalpha.com/article/4085232-6-dividend-investing-mistakes-avoid

10 Dividend Investing Mistakes to Avoid. (n.d.). Retrieved from https://www.dummies.com/personal-finance/investing/stocks-trading/10-dividend-investing-mistakes-to-avoid/

Dahle, J. (2018, November 12). Five Reasons to Avoid Focusing on Dividend Stocks. Retrieved from https://www.forbes.com/sites/jimdahle/2018/11/11/five-reasons-to-avoid-focusing-on-dividend-stocks/#1eb2627a7479

Frequently Asked Questions. (n.d.). Retrieved from https://www.dividendinvestor.com/faq/

Hanson, J. (2013, June 19). 7 Big Mistakes to Avoid in Stock Dividend Investing. Retrieved from https://www.thinkadvisor.com/2013/06/19/7-big-mistakes-to-avoid-in-stock-dividend-investin/?slreturn=20190524191739

Lichtenfeld, M. (2012). *Get rich with dividends a proven system for earning double-digit returns.* Hoboken, N.J.: Wiley.

O'Shea, A. (2019, June 18). High-Dividend Stocks: 25 Stocks That Pay High Yields. Retrieved from https://www.nerdwallet.com/blog/investing/high-dividend-stocks/

Royal, J., & O'shea, A. (2019, April 09). What Is a Dividend? Retrieved from https://www.nerdwallet.com/blog/investing/what-are-dividends/

What Are Dividends - FAQ. (n.d.). Retrieved from https://www.dividendearner.com/what-are-dividends-faq/

www.ingramcontent.com/pod-product-compliance
Lightning Source LLC
Chambersburg PA
CBHW070439180526
45158CB00019B/1741

* 9 7 8 1 0 8 8 4 5 6 7 5 0 *